Piano/Vocal Selections

Scott Landis, Roger Berlind, Sonia Friedman Productions, Roy Furm:
Standing CO Vation, Candy Spelling, Freddy DeMann, Ronald Frankel, Harold Newr
Raise the Roof 8, Takonkiet Viravan, William Berlind/Ed Burke, Carole L. Haber/!
Buddy and Barbara Freitag/Sanford Robertson, Jim Herbert/Under the '
Emanuel Azenberg, The Shubert Organization

PRESENT

Matthew Broderick   Kelli O'Hara

STARRING IN

If You Can Get It

A New Musical Comedy

MUSIC & LYRICS BY
George Gershwin and Ira Gershwin

BOOK BY
Joe DiPietro

Inspired by material by Guy Bolton and P.G. Wodehouse

ALSO STARRING
Michael McGrath   Jennifer Laura Thompson   Chris Sullivan
Robyn Hurder   Stanley Wayne Mathis   Terry Beaver

WITH
Judy Kaye

AND
Estelle Parsons

Cameron Adams   Clyde Alves   Kaitlyn Davidson   Jason DePinto   Kimberly Fauré
Robert Hartwell   Stephanie Martignetti   Barrett Martin   Michael X. Martin   Adam Perry   Jeffrey Schecter
Jennifer Smith   Joey Sorge   Samantha Sturm   Kristen Beth Williams   Candice Marie Woods

SCENIC DESIGN	COSTUME DESIGN	LIGHTING DESIGN	SOUND DESIGN
Derek McLane	Martin Pakledinaz	Peter Kaczorowski	Brian Ronan

HAIR & WIG DESIGN	MAKE-UP DESIGN	PROJECTION DESIGN	CASTING BY
Paul Huntley	Angelina Avallone	Alexander V. Nichols	Binder Casting Jay Binder/Jack Bowdan

ORCHESTRATOR	MUSIC DIRECTOR	MUSIC COORDINATOR	ASSOCIATE DIRECTOR	ASSOCIATE CHOREOGRAPHER
Bill Elliott	Tom Murray	Seymour Red Press	Marc Bruni	David Eggers

PRESS REPRESENTATIVE	ADVERTISING & MARKETING	TECHNICAL DIRECTOR	PRODUCTION STAGE MANAGER	GENERAL MANAGEMENT
Boneau/Bryan-Brown	Serino/Coyne	Neil Mazzella	Bonnie L. Becker	101 Productions, Ltd.

MUSIC SUPERVISION AND ARRANGEMENTS
David Chase

DIRECTED AND CHOREOGRAPHED BY
Kathleen Marshall

The worldwide copyrights in the works of George Gershwin and Ira Gershwin for this presentation are licensed by the Gershwin Family.

ISBN 978-1-4768-1677-7

7777 W. BLUEMOUND RD. P.O. BOX 13819 MILWAUKEE, WI 53213

In Australia Contact:
Hal Leonard Australia Pty. Ltd.
4 Lentara Court
Cheltenham, Victoria, 3192 Australia
Email: ausadmin@halleonard.com.au

Visit Hal Leonard Online at
www.halleonard.com

BLAH, BLAH, BLAH

Music and Lyrics by GEORGE GERSHWIN
and IRA GERSHWIN

BUT NOT FOR ME

Music and Lyrics by GEORGE GERSHWIN
and IRA GERSHWIN

BY STRAUSS

Music and Lyrics by GEORGE GERSHWIN
and IRA GERSWIN

DELISHIOUS

Music and Lyrics by GEORGE GERSHIWN
and IRA GERSHWIN

DEMON RUM

Music and Lyrics by GEORGE GERSHWIN
and IRA GERSHWIN

Lyrics:
De-mon rum, we'll ef-face you! De-mon rum, you dis-grace, you! You're an e-vil too man-y men crave! _____ Dev-il's brew!

DO-DO-DO

Music and Lyrics by GEORGE GERSHWIN
and IRA GERSHWIN

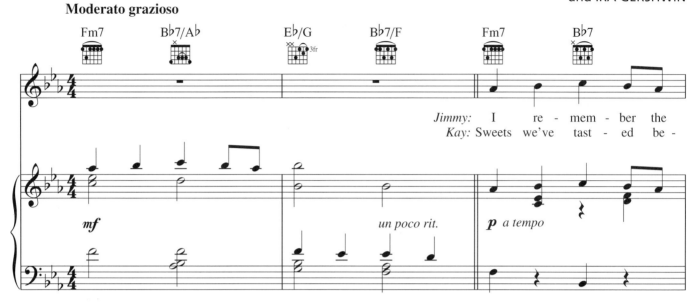

Jimmy: I re - mem - ber the
Kay: Sweets we've tast - ed be -

bliss   Of that won - der - ful kiss.   I knew that a
fore   Can - not stand an en - core.   You know that a

boy Could nev - er have more joy From an - y lit - tle miss.
miss Who al - ways gives a kiss Would soon be - come a bore.

DO IT AGAIN

Lyrics by B.G. DeSYLVA
Music by GEORGE GERSHWIN

FASCINATING RHYTHM

Music and Lyrics by GEORGE GERSHWIN
and IRA GERSHWIN

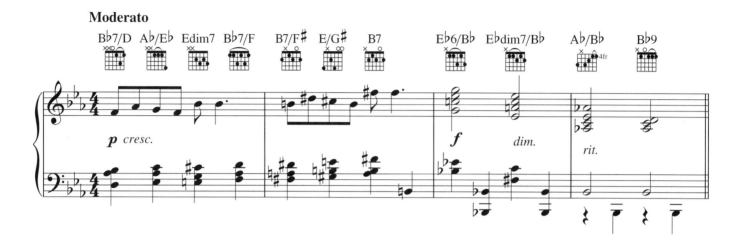

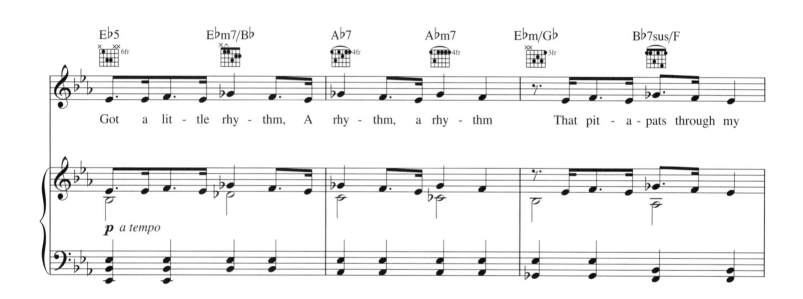

Got a lit - tle rhy - thm, A rhy - thm, a rhy - thm That pit - a - pats through my

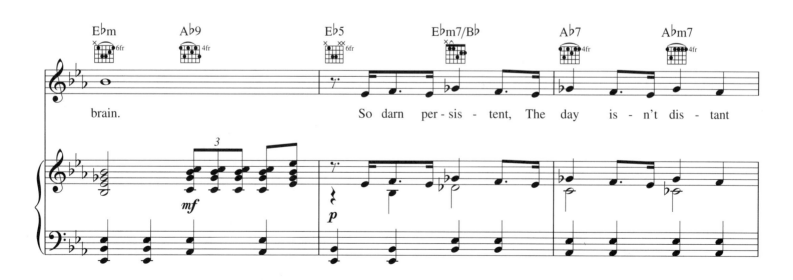

brain. So darn per - sis - tent, The day is - n't dis - tant

LET'S CALL THE WHOLE THING OFF

Music and Lyrics by GEORGE GERSHWIN
and IRA GERSHWIN

Allegretto

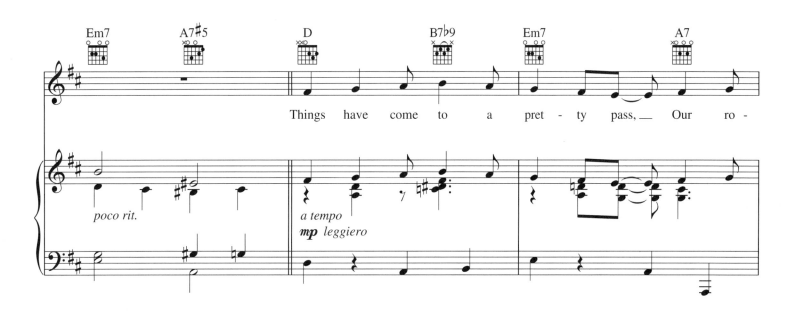

Things have come to a pret-ty pass, — Our ro-

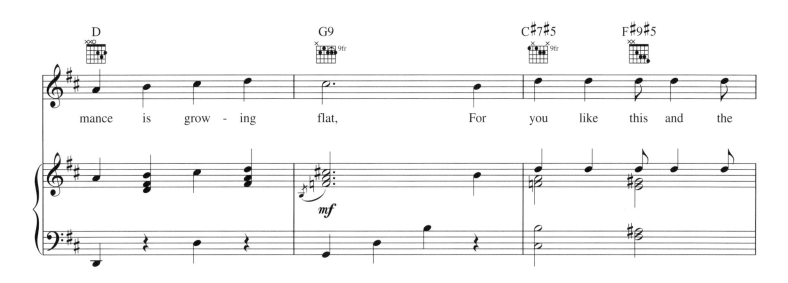

mance is grow-ing flat, For you like this and the

HANGIN' AROUND WITH YOU

Music and Lyrics by GEORGE GERSHWIN
and IRA GERSHWIN

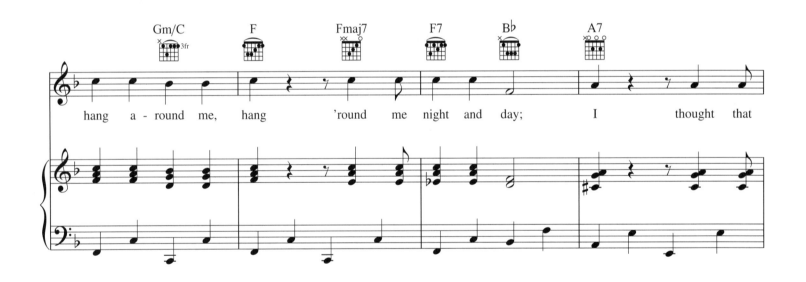

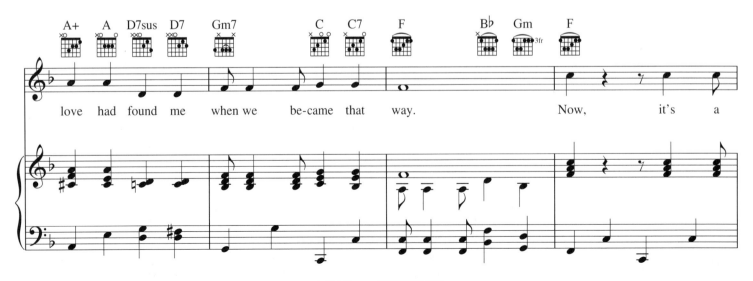

know. I'm be-gin-ning to see that I'm like-ly to

be on the shelf. If you want me hang-in' a-round with

you, hang-in' a-round with you, hang-in' a-round with you, dear - ie,

you've got to learn, you've got to learn to be your - self.

I'VE GOT A CRUSH ON YOU

Music and Lyrics by GEORGE GERSHWIN
and IRA GERSHWIN

Lightly, playfully

He: How
She: How

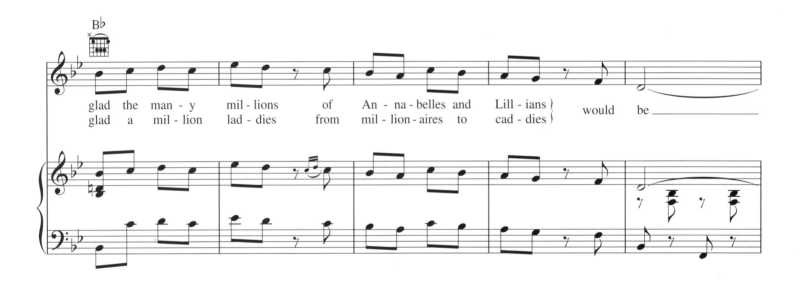

glad the man-y mil-lions of An-na-belles and Lill-ians } would be ____
glad a mil-lion lad-dies from mil-lion-aires to cad-dies }

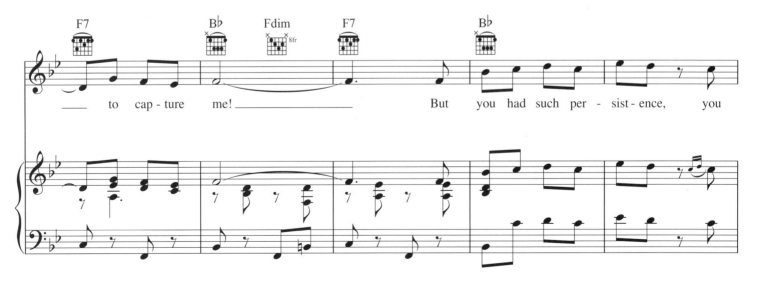

____ to cap-ture me! ____ But you had such per-sist-ence, you

I'VE GOT TO BE THERE

Music and Lyrics by GEORGE GERSHWIN
and IRA GERSHWIN

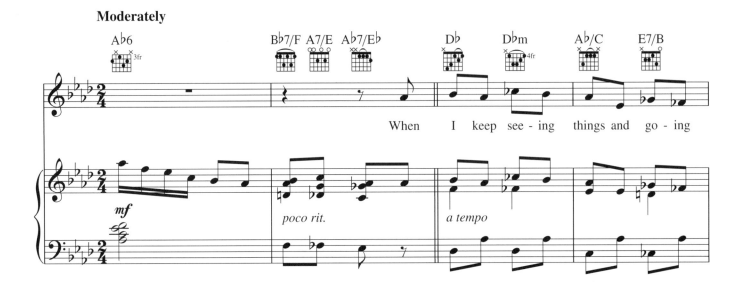

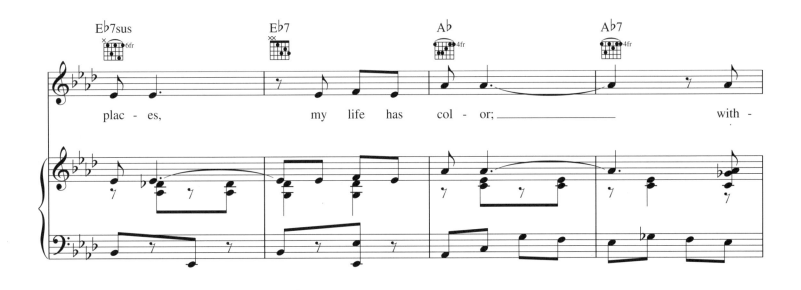

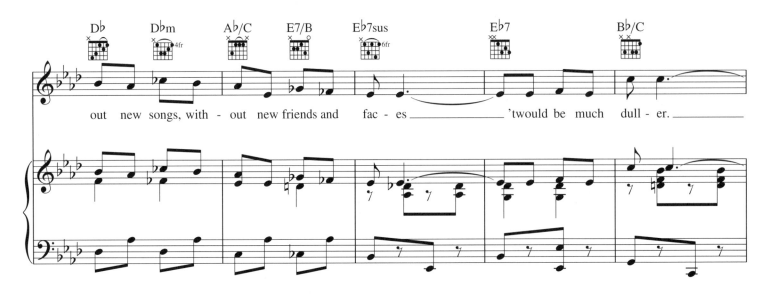

LOOKING FOR A BOY

Music and Lyrics by GEORGE GERSHWIN
and IRA GERSHWIN

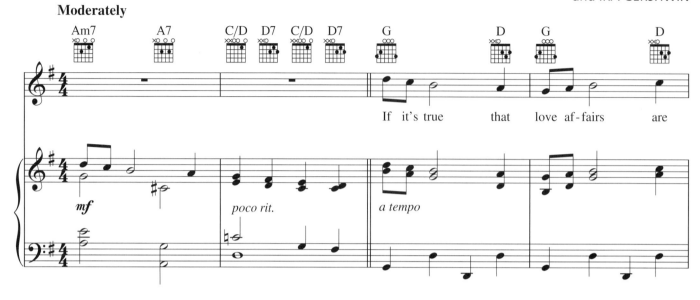

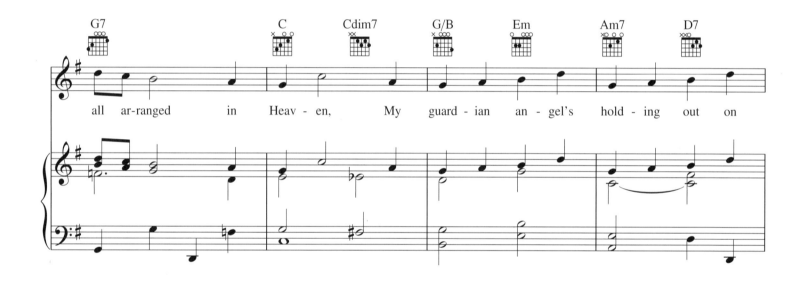

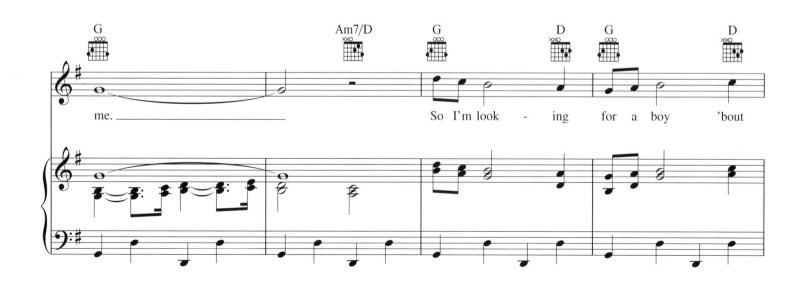

NICE WORK IF YOU CAN GET IT

Music and Lyrics by GEORGE GERSHWIN
and IRA GERSHWIN

SOMEONE TO WATCH OVER ME

Music and Lyrics by GEORGE GERSHWIN
and IRA GERSHWIN

'S WONDERFUL

Music and Lyrics by GEORGE GERSHWIN
and IRA GERSHWIN

SWEET AND LOW-DOWN

Music and Lyrics by GEORGE GERSHWIN
and IRA GERSHWIN

THEY ALL LAUGHED

Music and Lyrics by GEORGE GERSHWIN
and IRA GERSHWIN

THREE NOTE WALTZ

By GEORGE GERSHWIN

Moderate Waltz

WILL YOU REMEMBER ME?

Music and Lyrics by GEORGE GERSHWIN
and IRA GERSHWIN

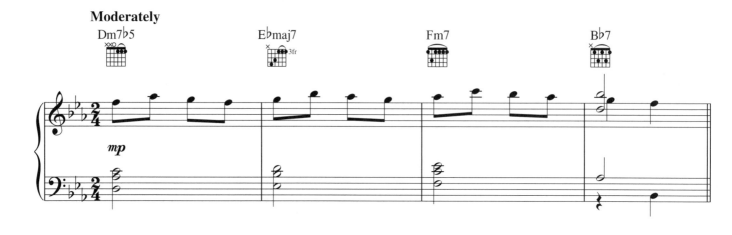

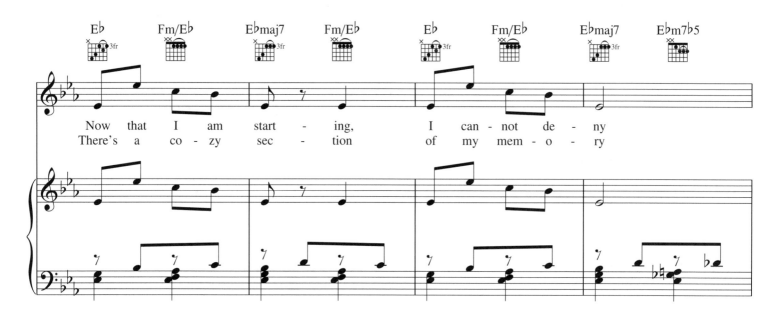

Now that I am start - ing, I can - not de - ny
There's a co - zy sec - tion of my mem - o - ry

I'd pre - fer a "see you lat - er" to a mere "good - bye."
I shall set a - side for you now that I've heard your plea.

TREAT ME ROUGH

Music and Lyrics by GEORGE GERSHWIN
and IRA GERSHWIN

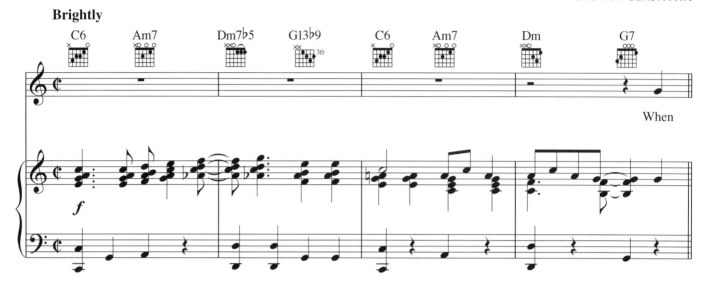

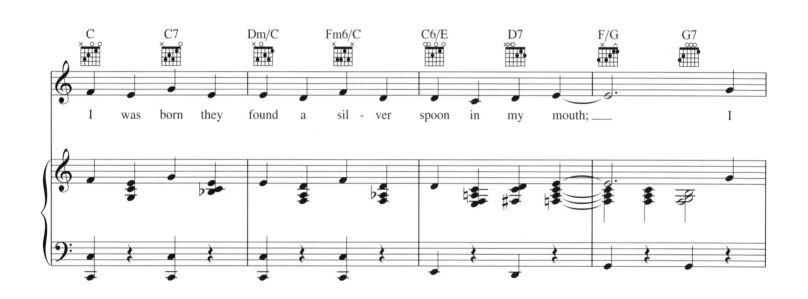

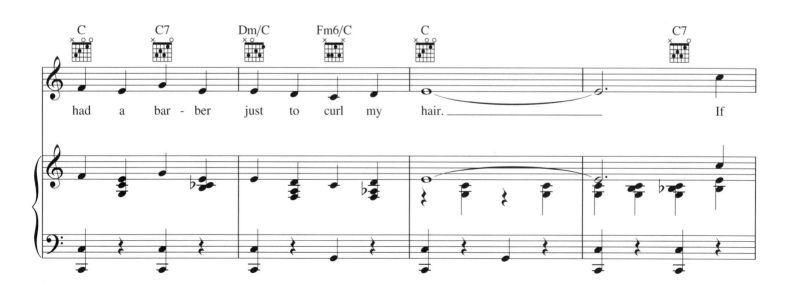